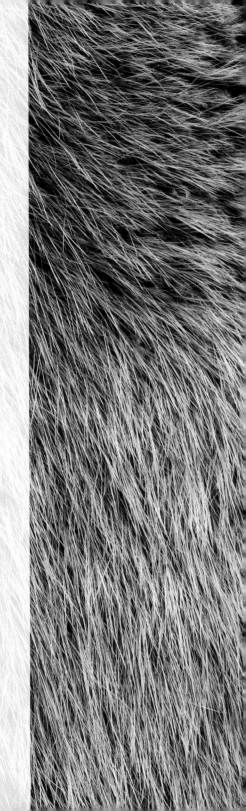

D1279389

TABLE OF CONTENTS

Hello,
beavers!

Beavers live in wooded places. They build dams in water.

A pond forms behind the dam. Beavers build a home there.

Beaver fur can
be brown or
black. The tail
is big and flat.

A beaver's back feet are webbed. This helps it swim.

Beavers have big front teeth. These orange teeth are sharp. Beavers chew through trees. They use the trees in the dam.

Hungry beavers eat wood and tree bark. They eat plants, too. Beavers store food for winter.

Kits are baby beavers. They drink milk and eat plants. Kits swim with their family.

Busy beavers work on their dams. They gather food at night. They dive underwater.

Goodbye,

beavers!

Picture a Beaver

ear

eye

nose

whiskers

teeth

fur

claw

back foot

tail

Words to Know

dams: barriers across a river or stream made of trees, branches, and other natural materials

fur: the short, hairy coat of an animal

webbed: connected with flexible skin

22

Read More

Johnson, Jinny. *Beaver*.
Mankato, Minn.: Smart Apple Media, 2014.

Riggs, Kate. *Beavers*.
Mankato, Minn.: Creative Education, 2015.

Websites

National Geographic Kids: Beaver
http://kids.nationalgeographic.com/animals
/beaver/#beaver-closeup.jpg
Learn more about busy beaver families.

PBS: Leave it to Beavers
https://www.youtube.com/watch?v=yJjaQExOPPY
Watch a video to see how beavers build dams.

Note: Every effort has been made to ensure that the websites listed above are suitable for children, that they have educational value, and that they contain no inappropriate material. However, because of the nature of the Internet, it is impossible to guarantee that these sites will remain active indefinitely or that their contents will not be altered.

23

Index